The Chinese Thought of It

豬

The Chinese Thought of It

AMAZING INVENTIONS AND INNOVATIONS

Ting-xing Ye

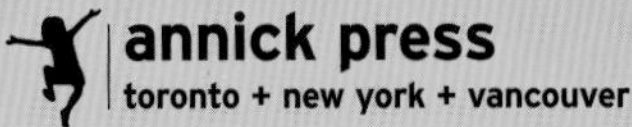

Cover illustration by David Craig
Cover and interior design by Sheryl Shapiro
Edited by David MacDonald
Map on pages 10–11 by Tina Holdcroft

Annick Press Ltd.

We acknowledge the support of the Canada Council for the Arts, the Ontario Arts Council, and the Government of Canada through the Book Publishing Industry Development Program (BPIDP) for our publishing activities.

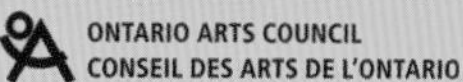

A sincere thank-you to expert reader Francesca Bray, Professor of Social Anthropology, University of Edinburgh, for her time and efforts.

Cataloging in Publication

Ye, Ting-xing, 1952-
The Chinese thought of it : amazing inventions and innovations / Ting-xing Ye.

(We thought of it)
Includes bibliographical references and index.
ISBN 978-1-55451-196-9 (bound).—ISBN 978-1-55451-195-2 (pbk.)

1. Inventions—China—History—Juvenile literature.
2. Technology—China—History—Juvenile literature.
3. China—Antiquities—Juvenile literature. I. Title.
II. Series: We thought of it

T27.C5Y42 2009 j609.51 C2009-903078-0

Distributed in Canada by:
Firefly Books Ltd.
66 Leek Crescent
Richmond Hill, ON
L4B 1H1

Published in the U.S.A. by:
Annick Press (U.S.) Ltd.
Distributed in the U.S.A. by:
Firefly Books (U.S.) Inc.
P.O. Box 1338
Ellicott Station
Buffalo, NY 14205

Watch for more books in the We Thought of It series, coming soon.

Printed in China.

Visit us at: www.annickpress.com

For Bella, William, and Seamus. May this book be your first step toward China.
—T.Y.

Contents

Huan ying, Welcome

Qian-li-zhi-xing, shi-yu-zu-xia.

Even the longest journey begins with the first step.

I welcome you on this journey to discover the amazing inventions and innovations of ancient China. You probably guessed from my name that I am Chinese. I was born and raised in Shanghai, where I lived for many years before I came to Canada. When I was a kid, I went to school like you. I learned to read, write, and do arithmetic. Later on, I took on History, Geography, Science, and other subjects.

Top and bottom: Views of the Forbidden City, where emperors once lived

I studied English at Beijing University. My second language helped me understand the world better. After graduation, I worked as an English interpreter for many years. During that time I met many leaders from other countries, including members of the Canadian Parliament and the American Congress.

I thought I knew a lot about China's past and present. It wasn't until I sat down to write this book that I realized I had much more to learn. As I got deeper into my research, reading books and checking Internet resources, I grew more and more excited about my findings. I am glad I have the chance to share with you what I have learned. I hope this book will be the beginning

The skyline of Shanghai, China's largest city

of your own journey of discovery. Now, let's take the first step together.

China is the third largest country in the world, after Canada and Russia. In the north is a great plain. To the south are rivers, lakes, and lowlands. In the west are mountains. China's two great rivers, the Long River, or Yangtze, and the Yellow River are among the longest in the world.

Computer games are popular in modern China.

Some of ancient China's famous inventions are still used today, in China and around the world. Many of them have been improved; many remain the same.

When I was a teenager, the Chinese government forced millions of people my age to go and live in the countryside. At sixteen, I was sent to work

The Great Wall of China

on a farm far from home. The main crop there was rice. Each spring we used iron plows pulled by water buffalo to turn up the hardened earth before the fields were flooded to make paddies. Later, I and other teenagers hand-planted rice seedlings in straight rows, following an ancient method I describe in this book. The grid we formed made weeding and harvesting a lot easier and more efficient.

On the farm, the wheelbarrow was one of our main transportation tools. We used it to haul bricks, bags of grain and fertilizer, and once even a newborn calf. I learned from experience that wheelbarrows with longer handles were easier to control and required less strength when pushing a heavy load. That was a good thing because I was a small and light young woman at that time. My farm-mates and I fondly called our wheelbarrows "wooden oxen."

Zhangjiajie National Forest Park

Statues of warriors and horses discovered near the tomb of China's first emperor

Apart from the iron plow and wheelbarrow, my research brought back even more memories: the type of yokes and harnesses placed on the farm animals, the hoes we used in the vegetable garden, and the herbal medicine we were given at the village clinic. All these things were invented by the ancient Chinese. All are still very useful.

I hope you will find your journey of discovery interesting. Enjoy your trip.

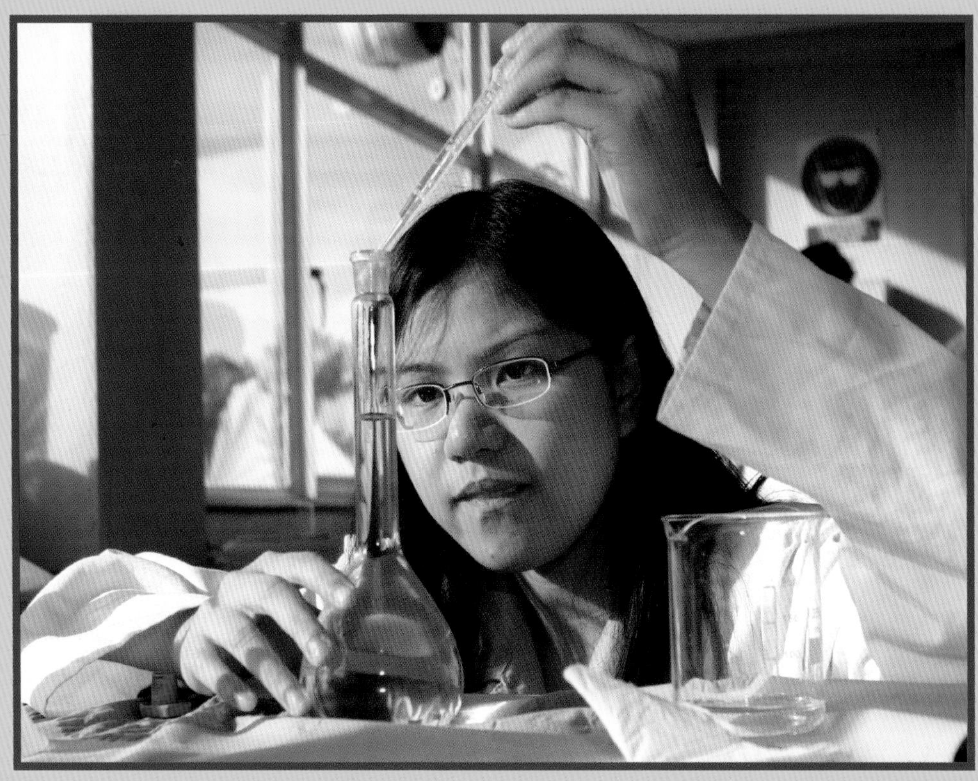

A medical student at work in a lab

MAP OF CHINA TODAY

Gobi Desert
Beijing
Tianjin
Bo Hai
Sea
Yellow River
Yellow
Sea
Xi'an
Nanjing
Shanghai
Wuhan
Hangzhou
East
China
Sea
Chongqing
Yangtze River
Guangzhou
Hong Kong
South China Sea

TIMELINE

Chinese civilization stretches back to prehistoric times. Scholars divide this long history into time periods. Most of these periods are named for a dynasty—a line of rulers who all belonged to the same family.

This timeline shows some of the major Chinese dynasties. Experts disagree about the exact dates for some dynasties.

Bronze vase from the Han dynasty

Shang Dynasty
1650–1100 BCE

Zhou Dynasty
1100–221 BCE

Qin Dynasty
221–207 BCE

Han Dynasty
207 BCE–220 CE

Period of Disunity
220–581 CE

Sui Dynasty
581–618 CE

Tang Dynasty
618–907 CE

Reproduction of a gold bowl from the Tang dynasty

A Note on Dates

Dates are identified as BCE (Before Common Era) and CE (Common Era). Numbers for BCE years get larger when moving into the past—for example, the year 10 BCE is more recent than 20 BCE. Dates for CE years get smaller when moving into the past—20 CE is more recent than 10 CE.

1000 BCE **500 BCE** **500 CE** **1000 CE**

Dragon wall decoration from the Qing dynasty

Five Dynasties
907–960 CE

Song Dynasty
960–1279 CE

Yuan Dynasty
1279–1368 CE

Ming Dynasty
1368–1644 CE

Qing Dynasty
1644–1912 CE

Republic
1912–Present

Pagoda from the Song dynasty

Ceramic figurine from the Ming dynasty

FARMING

In China, only 10 percent of the land is suitable for farming. In order to feed the large and fast-growing population of ancient times, the Chinese came up with many inventions and innovations that helped to produce more food.

In this field, rice has been planted in vertical and horizontal rows that form a grid.

Planting in Rows

Plants that are too close together in the field will not grow as quickly as plants that are spaced apart. The Chinese were the first to plant crops in vertical and horizontal rows (a grid pattern), which left more room around each plant.

By the 6th century BCE, Chinese farmers were planting rice, soybeans, and other important crops in rows. A text written in the 3rd century BCE explains, "If the crops are grown in rows, they will mature rapidly because they will not interfere with each other's development. The horizontal rows must be well drawn, the vertical rows made with skill, for if the lines are straight the wind will pass gently through." This planting method is still used today.

Intensive Hoeing

Hoeing, or loosening the soil around a plant, helps crops grow. It lets air get down into the soil and allows the ground to hold moisture better.

The innovation of planting in rows that formed a grid enabled farmers to hoe around each plant without causing any damage. This technique is known as intensive hoeing.

Swan-Neck Hoe

The Chinese created a variety of hoe designs, which in turn led to better harvests. Around the 1st century BCE, they developed the swan-neck hoe. The part of the hoe above the blade was curved like the neck of a swan. This allowed farmers to stand in one place and hoe all around a plant without damaging it.

Swan-neck hoes are still popular today in China and around the world.

Wheelbarrow

Historians believe that the wheelbarrow (called a "single-wheeled cart" in Chinese) was invented in southwestern China in the 1st century BCE. It was made of wood and had one large wheel. The benefit of this invention was that it allowed a single person to move a heavy load. Wheelbarrows were important not only in rural areas. In times of war, they were used to carry supplies to troops. This simple invention helped the ancient Chinese win many battles.

Iron Plowshare

A plowshare is the main cutting blade of a plow. It digs a shallow furrow, or trench, when the plow is dragged across a field by a horse or an ox. Around the 6th century BCE, the Chinese replaced stone plowshares with ones made of bronze or iron. These were the first metal plowshares in the world. By the 3rd century BCE, improved iron supplies and casting techniques (see page 16) produced bigger plowshares that were able to make deeper furrows in various types of soil and break up the soil more effectively.

Harness

A harness is a set of straps fastened to an animal, such as a horse or an ox, so it can pull a heavy load. The earliest harnesses had a strap that went around the animal's throat. But this design could cause choking.

In the 4th century BCE, the Chinese developed the trace harness. It had a strap that went across the animal's chest so it did not choke.

Around the 1st century BCE, the Chinese came up with a better design, called a collar harness. A thick, padded collar went around the animal's chest and shoulders. Because a collar harness made it possible for one horse or ox to pull a heavier load, fewer animals were needed. This helped farmers produce more food.

With a trace harness, the horse did not choke.

The dragon-spine water lift helped farmers irrigate their crops.

Dragon-Spine Water Lift

Water is very important to farming. In ancient China, fetching water from a river was a backbreaking chore, mainly done by carrying water in buckets.

In the 1st century CE, the Chinese invented the first chain pump, called the dragon-spine water lift. It got this name because it had a wooden circulating chain, which worked similarly to the chain on a bicycle. Many squares made from wood were evenly spaced along the chain. These reminded people of the spine of a dragon, an important animal in Chinese mythology.

On this water lift, people used their feet to work treadles, much like pedaling a bicycle. The pieces of wood attached to the chain pulled water up from a river, through a wooden trough, and then dumped it into a field or reservoir. In some places, similar chain pumps are still used today.

WORKING WITH METAL

The Chinese were the first to invent certain processes for working with metal, and were able to produce large quantities of metal objects.

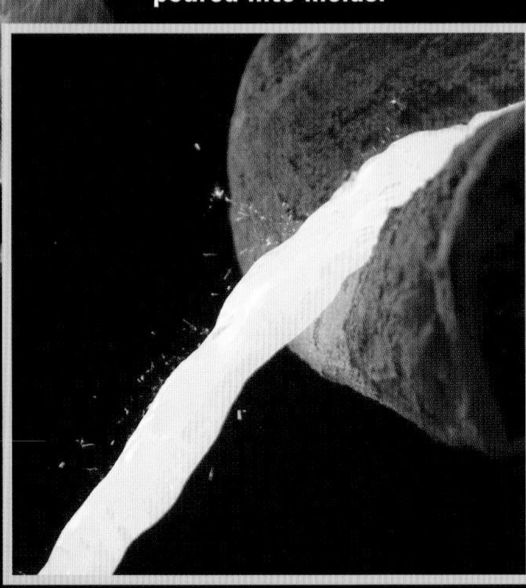

To make cast iron, the metal is melted and then poured into molds.

Cast Iron

Iron is a silver-white metal found in ore (a mixture of metal and rock). Heating the ore separates the iron from the rock. This kind of iron is quite soft and bends easily. As early as the 6th century BCE, the Chinese invented a way to make iron stronger. This new method produced cast iron, and it was used to make such things as cooking pots, knives, axes, statues, and even toys.

福

Double-acting piston bellows are still used today in wood-burning or straw-burning stoves in rural China.

Double-Acting Piston Bellows

A bellows forces air into a fire to make it hotter. In its most familiar form, a bellows has two handles that are squeezed together to push out the air inside. When the handles are pulled apart, air is drawn back in.

In ancient China, a bellows was used to make the fire inside a furnace hot enough to melt iron. Around the 4th century BCE, the Chinese developed the double-acting piston bellows. This new invention forced out a continuous stream of air as the handle was pushed in and pulled out. This made fires hotter than was possible with bellows that produced short puffs of air.

Double-acting piston bellows can still be found in rural China, where they are sometimes called "push-and-pull bellows."

Earthquake Detector

The world's first earthquake detector was invented in 132 CE by a Chinese astronomer named Zhang Heng. His invention was a huge cast-bronze jar 2 meters (6 feet) across, with a domed lid. Eight dragon heads were spaced along the outside of the jar, each holding a bronze ball in its jaws. Directly under each dragon head was a bronze toad with its mouth open. An earthquake caused a rod inside the jar to push the ball out of a dragon's jaws and into the mouth of the toad below it. This created a loud *bong* to alert people. The toad with the fallen ball showed the direction of the earthquake.

The ancient Chinese earthquake detector (below, left) was invented many centuries before the seismograph (above), which modern scientists use to detect and measure earthquakes.

Mechanical Clock

A Chinese Buddhist monk and mathematician named Yi Xing invented the first mechanical clock. It was completed in 725 CE.

Unlike the clocks we have today, which have hands and a dial, this clock was an astronomical instrument. It showed the movement of the earth, sun, and moon. Along with measuring longer periods of time, such as a day and a year, it also had a bell that rang each hour and a drum that sounded every 15 minutes.

The clock was powered by a waterwheel. Water flowing into scoops on a huge wheel made it turn. The mechanism of this clock was made of bronze and iron.

In 1092 CE, an astronomer named Su Song built an even more complicated version. It required a tower more than 9 meters (30 feet) tall to contain the clock and its mechanism.

The clock was not only one of the most incredible mechanical inventions of its time, it also showed the ability of the ancient Chinese to work with metal.

Su Song's mechanical clock

The Chinese used metal in many other inventions and innovations. See also Swan-Neck Hoe (page 14), Iron Plowshare (page 15), Compass (page 18), Stirrups (page 23), and Crossbow (page 23).

TRANSPORTATION AND EXPLORATION

喜

Transporting people and goods from place to place is important in any culture. The ancient Chinese came up with inventions that made transportation—and exploration—much easier.

Compass

Sometime before the 4th century BCE, the Chinese discovered magnetism. This knowledge helped them to invent the compass, which uses a magnetized object to indicate a direction. Unlike the compass we know, which points north, a Chinese compass points south. The Chinese call it a "south-pointing needle."

Because compasses tell people if they are heading in the right direction, they were very important for transportation and exploration. They were especially useful on ships on cloudy days and nights when sailors couldn't use the sun or stars to help them navigate.

A Chinese compass from the 19th century CE

Watertight Compartments in Ships

As early as the 2nd century CE, the Chinese were building ships with watertight compartments below the deck. If an accident caused a hole in the ship, only one of these compartments would fill with water, so the ship would not sink. And if a cargo ship sprang a leak, only the goods in one compartment would be damaged.

Paddle-Wheel Boat

Paddle-wheel boats get their power from paddle wheels, rather than oars or sails. In the 5th century CE, the Chinese were the first to build a paddle-wheel boat. At that time, the wheel was turned by people working inside the boat.

The design of these boats improved over time. Some had more than one paddle wheel, which allowed them to travel faster. Later, larger paddle-wheel ships were built for battle. In the 12th century CE, some paddle-wheel ships had as many as 23 wheels and could carry 200 to 300 people.

A modern paddle wheel

A paddle wheel is visible on this life-size marble replica of a boat at the Summer Palace in Beijing.

Rudder

Long ago, sailors in all cultures used an oar to steer ships. This oar was usually attached to the side of a ship, near the stern (back of the ship). Some ships had a steering oar on each side.

This rudder is on a modern boat.

The steering oar had several disadvantages. It didn't always work very well, especially on a large ship. Before 100 CE, the Chinese invented the rudder. It was a large blade attached to the stern. Most of the rudder was under the surface of the water.

The rudder was much easier to use than a steering oar. It accurately controlled the direction of the ship, and worked well on both large and small boats.

The Chinese also invented a rudder that had holes in it to let water flow through. This made it easier for the rudder to move back and forth in the water.

Masts and Sails

The Chinese were the first to use sails on ships. Modern sails are made of cloth, but early Chinese sails were usually made of bamboo strips with woven bamboo mats stretched between them. These sails could be pulled up or down like window blinds, which made sailing in rough weather easier. They also allowed sailors to operate the sails from the deck without climbing up the masts, which are tall poles attached to the ship's frame.

The Chinese were also the first to use "staggered masts"—masts that were placed in a zigzag arrangement rather than in a straight line. This allowed the ship to sail into the wind, rather than always with the wind.

CANALS AND BRIDGES

Apart from being the main source of water for drinking and irrigation, rivers provide important transportation routes. The ancient Chinese were the first to create contour transport canals. They also invented ways to build different kinds of bridges.

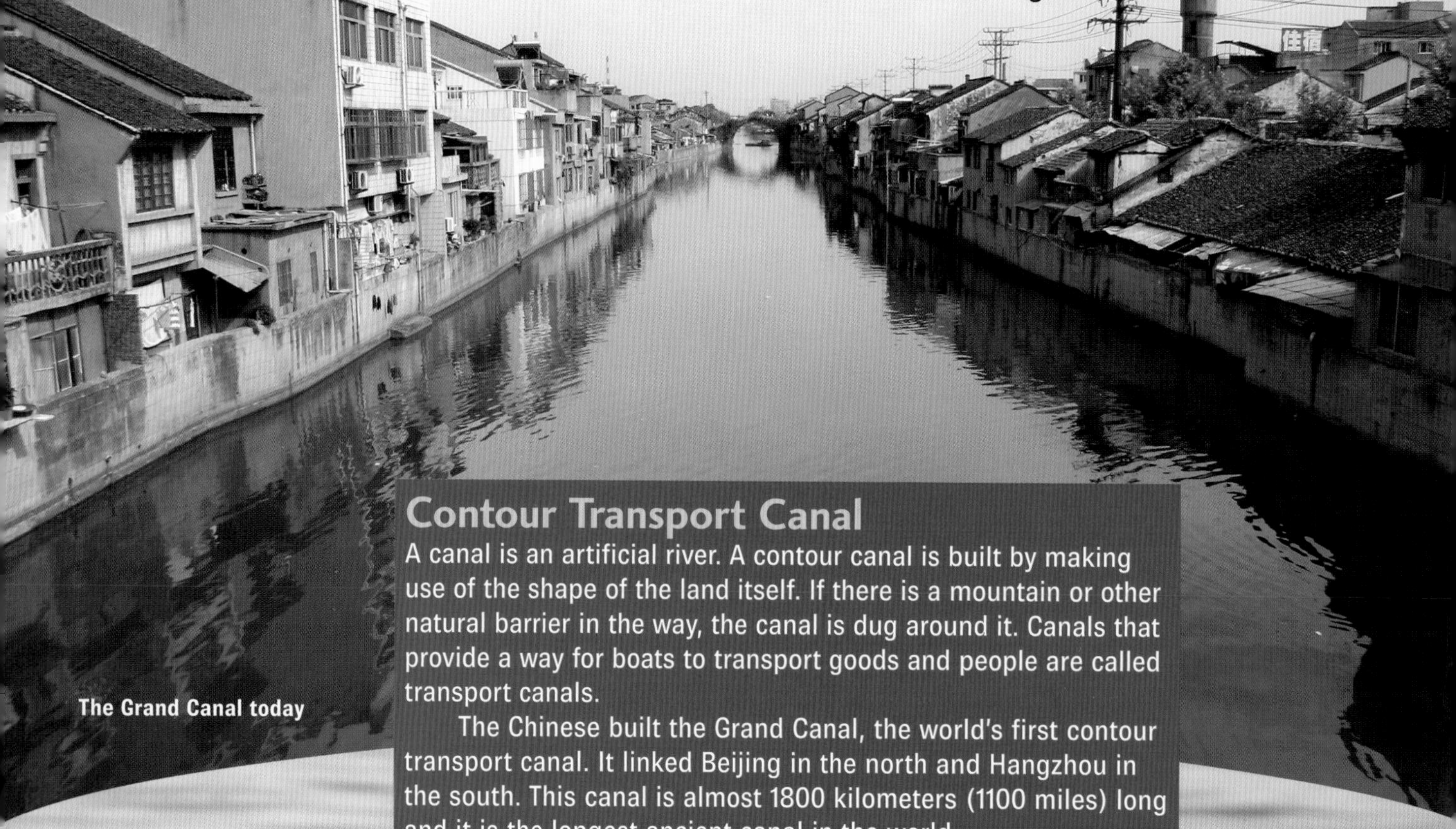

The Grand Canal today

Contour Transport Canal

A canal is an artificial river. A contour canal is built by making use of the shape of the land itself. If there is a mountain or other natural barrier in the way, the canal is dug around it. Canals that provide a way for boats to transport goods and people are called transport canals.

The Chinese built the Grand Canal, the world's first contour transport canal. It linked Beijing in the north and Hangzhou in the south. This canal is almost 1800 kilometers (1100 miles) long and it is the longest ancient canal in the world.

Pound Lock

How can you travel uphill on a canal? The answer is to create a pound lock. A pound lock has two sets of watertight gates. When a boat approaches from the lower part of the canal, one set of gates opens to let the boat in, and then the gates close. Water from the higher part of the canal is gradually let into the lock until the water rises to the same level as the upper canal. Then the upper gates open and the boat leaves the lock. The procedure is reversed for boats making the downhill journey.

The first pound lock was built in China in the 10th century CE. Similar but much larger locks operate today at the Three Gorges Dam on the Yangtze River.

A pound lock at the Three Gorges Dam

Suspension Bridge

The suspension bridge is one of the oldest types of bridges. In ancient times, simple forms of suspension footbridges were used by many cultures around the world. They were made from twisted ropes and vines, and people walked directly on the ropes. Around 285 BCE, the Chinese built the first suspension bridge that had a platform made from planks resting on bamboo cables.

Today, huge suspension bridges have a roadbed suspended from cables attached to a steel frame or concrete towers for support.

Suspension footbridges are still in use around the world.

A semicircular arch bridge in Shanghai during the 1860s CE

Segmental Arch Bridge

An arch is a curved structure that extends over an opening in a bridge or building. It can hold up a great deal of weight. The arches of ancient bridges were shaped like a semicircle (half a circle). In the 7th century CE, a Chinese engineer realized that a bridge arch could be in the form of a small portion of a semicircle. This is called a segmental arch. The first segmental arch bridge was built in China.

The most famous segmental arch bridge is the Marco Polo Bridge, built in 1189 CE in the west of Beijing. It has a series of eleven segmental arches. Today the world's longest segmental arch bridge is the Lupu Bridge in Shanghai, China, constructed in 2003, which uses just one arch.

A segmental arch bridge

Pontoon Bridge

A pontoon bridge floats on water, with each end attached to the shore. It is usually a temporary bridge. The earliest record of a pontoon bridge comes from China, in the Zhou dynasty (1100–221 BCE). King Wen ordered boats to be joined together to form a floating bridge.

安

WEAPONS AND WARFARE

Several important military inventions and innovations, from horse stirrups to gunpowder, came from China. Weapons made of metal, such as the crossbow, were produced in large numbers.

Gunpowder

Gunpowder (called "fire medicine" in Chinese) was invented in the 9th century CE. The inventors were trying to find a medicine that would let people live forever. Instead, they created something that would be used in war.

The development of gunpowder took place over many centuries. Eventually, it was used to make weapons. One was a bomb that burned rather than exploded. When it struck a wooden structure, it started a fire and gave off poison gas. Another terrifying Chinese invention was the flame-thrower, which sprayed enemies with burning oil.

In the 11th century CE, the Chinese used gunpowder to make a variety of explosive weapons.

Gunpowder burns quickly and causes explosions.

Spectacular fireworks marked the opening ceremonies of the 2008 Olympic Games in Beijing.

Firecrackers and Fireworks

Around the 10th century CE, the Chinese used gunpowder to invent firecrackers and fireworks.

Firecrackers (called "crackling cannons" in Chinese) are made from paper tubes filled with gunpowder. When the fuse is lit, the tube blows up with a loud bang.

In ancient China, firecrackers were used to scare off enemies and horses in battle. Some Chinese also believed that the loud explosion would chase away evil spirits.

The Chinese have long been considered experts at making fireworks. The early forms produced only a loud bang and a puff of smoke, which may be why fireworks are called "smoke flowers" in Chinese. Today, people around the world enjoy beautiful fireworks displays in times of celebration.

Military Manual

A military manual is a book that gives advice about how to fight and win battles. The oldest military manual in the world, *The Art of War*, was written in China around the 5th century BCE by Sun Zi (also known as Sun Tzu). This book discusses military strategy, and gives other kinds of advice as well.

Today, the book is read and studied all over the world. People outside the military also find it useful in sports and business.

In this Qing dynasty copy of *The Art of War*, the text is written on strips of bamboo.

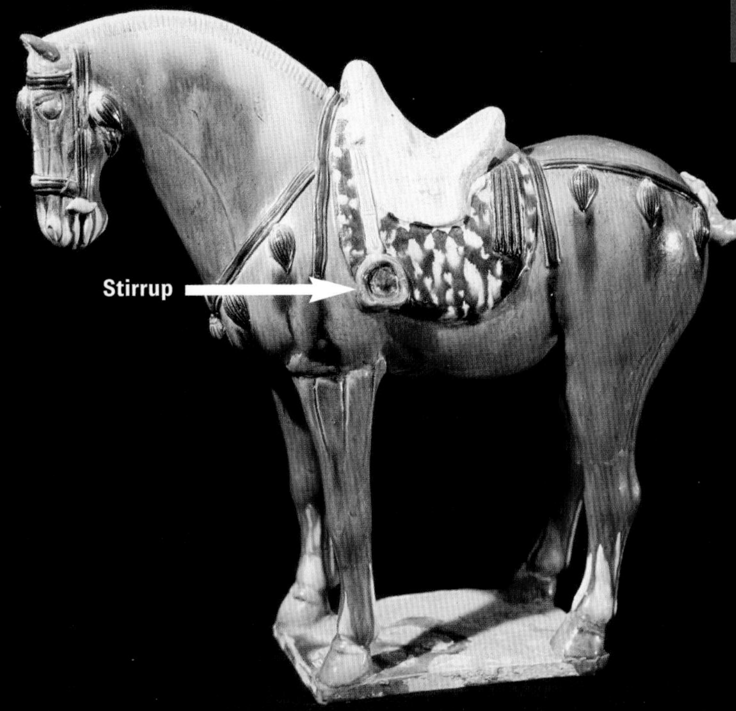

Stirrups

A stirrup is a metal ring with a flat bottom. One stirrup hangs from each side of a saddle so that the rider of a horse has a place to rest his feet. The Chinese came up with this simple but very important device in the 3rd century CE.

Before the stirrup was invented, it was difficult to mount a horse and the rider had no support for his feet. He had to hold onto the horse's mane and squeeze with both legs to avoid falling off. With his feet in the stirrups, a rider could hold and use weapons. It was also harder for an enemy to knock him off his horse.

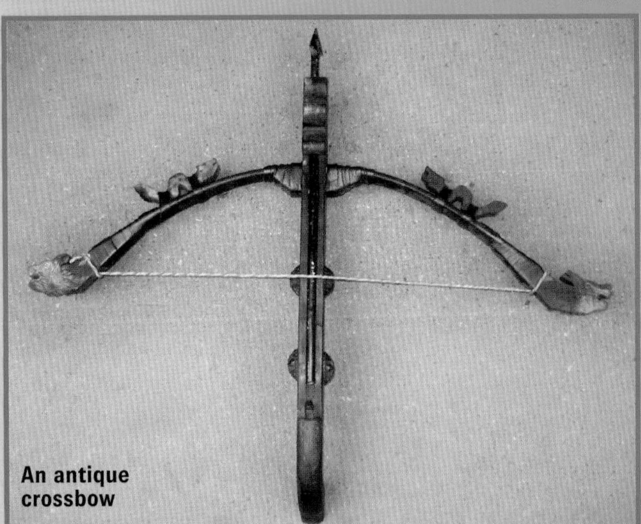

An antique crossbow

Crossbow

The crossbow was invented in China in the 4th century BCE and was the standard weapon used by Chinese troops for over 2000 years. It shot a bolt (a short, heavy arrow) with great force, and a soldier could learn to use it in just a couple of weeks.

The Chinese also invented the repeating crossbow. This weapon allowed a soldier to string the bow, place the bolt, and shoot, all with one hand. This meant that soldiers could shoot more quickly—as many as 11 bolts in 15 seconds.

PAPER AND PRINTING

Paper is one of the greatest inventions of ancient China. Imagine how different our life would be without paper! The Chinese also invented methods of printing, which created the first paper money in the world.

Making Paper

The ancient Egyptians created a writing surface by pressing together strips of papyrus plant. But it wasn't paper.

Paper was first made by the Chinese around the 2nd century BCE. The method they used was similar to the one we use today. But instead of using wood, they used hemp plants, mulberry bark, bamboo, silk rags, or rice straw.

In papermaking, the material was pounded until it disintegrated. Then liquid was added to make it into a pulp. Next, the pulp was spread evenly on top of a fabric screen or a mold, which let the liquid drain through. The dried pulp was paper. It was easily peeled off the mold or screen.

In a tomb in northwest China, archaeologists discovered a piece of paper that had been made sometime between 140 and 87 BCE. It is the oldest paper ever found.

A 17th-century worker makes paper.

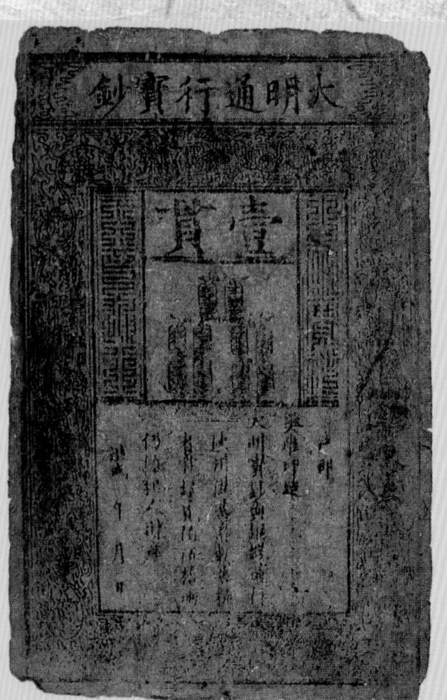

Paper money from the Ming dynasty

Paper Money

The Chinese invention of paper and printing led to the world's first paper money.

Ancient Chinese coins were made of copper or bronze and had a square hole in the middle. This allowed many coins to be strung together, but the strings of coins were heavy to carry, especially for traveling merchants.

To get around these difficulties, merchants left coins with a local business. In return, they received a handwritten note indicating the amount of money they had deposited. When they traveled to a different place, they took the note with them. They showed the note to a local business and got back the same amount of money they had deposited earlier.

By 1000 CE, people received printed notes instead of handwritten notes when they deposited coins. This was the first printed paper money. The Chinese called these notes "flying money" because they were so much lighter than coins.

This scene was printed on Chinese wallpaper during the Qing dynasty.

How People Used Paper

Because of the materials the Chinese used, early paper was thick and rough and wasn't good for writing. Instead, it was used for wrapping delicate objects, packaging medicine, and for clothing. Later it was used to make military armor. The paper was folded in pleats, with layers of cloth or silk fabric. This armor provided strong protection from arrows and even bullets.

People made curtains and blankets from paper, and also used it as wall covering—wallpaper is another Chinese invention. Paper was also used for artistic activities such as papercutting and origami (see page 27).

Early Chinese toilet paper was not as soft and smooth as this modern toilet paper.

Toilet Paper

Around the 6th century CE, the Chinese invented toilet paper. Because it was made from rice straw, it was very rough. Today, many Chinese still call toilet paper "straw paper," even though it is no longer made from straw. During the Ming dynasty (1368–1644 CE), the emperor and his family had toilet paper that was soft and sometimes even perfumed.

Writing Paper

The quality of paper improved in the years after it was invented. But it took nearly 100 years before people began to write on it. The oldest piece of paper with words written on it was discovered in China in 1942. It was about 1900 years old.

Before people wrote and printed books on paper, they used silk or strips of bamboo. (See page 23 for photos of a book written on bamboo strips.)

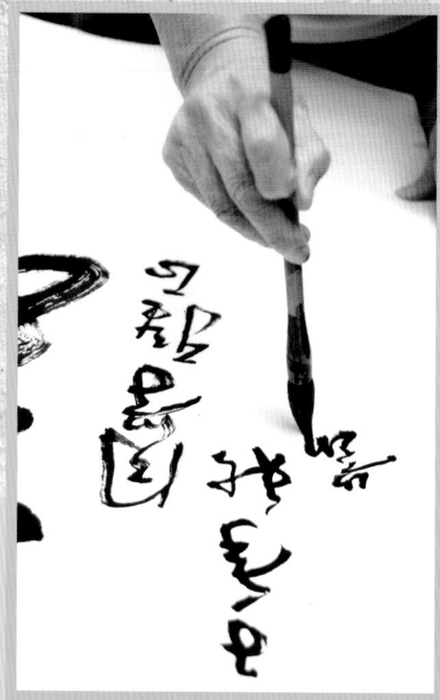

Traditional Chinese writing is done with a brush.

Woodblock Printing

The woodblock printing method was invented by the Chinese around the 7th century CE to meet the growing need for more than one copy of written material.

This method started with a block of wood that had a smooth surface. To make a woodblock for printing, people first wrote the text in ink on a sheet of paper. Then they pressed the inked side of the paper on top of the block, leaving a mirror image of the text on the surface of the block. All the wood around each word was carved away. To create a printed page, the raised words on the block were brushed with ink. A blank page was pressed onto the block, then peeled off. The first book was printed in this way in 868 CE.

A carved woodblock

Carved cubes for moveable type printing

Moveable Type Printing

Around 1041–1048 CE in China, a man named Bi Sheng invented a new printing method. It was called moveable type printing.

Unlike a printing woodblock, which took a lot of time to prepare and allowed no mistakes, the new invention used small cubes made from slightly wet clay. Bi Sheng carved one Chinese character, or word, on each cube, then baked the cubes in fire until they were dry. He made many copies of each word. When he wished to print, he selected the cubes he needed and set them inside a frame, which formed a page of text. Then, he pressed a piece of paper on the inked cubes. These blocks could be used over and over again. Movable type made printing quick and easy.

Papercutting

Papercutting is a craft that was created in China soon after the invention of paper. Several layers of paper were fastened together and cut to create artistic designs or pictures.

This art form is still popular in China. The finished cuttings are mainly used for decoration during special occasions, such as Chinese New Year or weddings. Red paper is often used and the cuttings are pasted on walls, doors and windows. People in northern China have a special name for the decorative red papercuttings placed on windows—they call them "window flowers."

Modern examples of the traditional art of papercutting

Modern examples of origami

Origami

Origami is a Japanese word for the art of folding paper into shapes that look like flowers, birds, or other objects. It is likely that origami first started in China, since paper was invented there. Today, origami is a popular art form around the world.

SILK

This piece of woven silk was made in 551 CE.

Silk is one of the most famous discoveries of ancient China. Fabric made from woven silk threads is strong and beautiful. The secret of how to make this precious material was closely guarded. The Chinese did not want the rest of the world to find out how to make silk.

At first, silk was so rare that only members of important families wore silk clothes. Later, when silk production became an industry, silk clothing became available to more people.

Today, silk is available in almost any color you can imagine.

Steps for Making Silk

Making silk is a slow process and requires great care. Over time, the ancient Chinese perfected the method for silk production.

STEP 1: The eggs from a silkmoth are kept in an environment where the temperature is carefully controlled. Silkworms hatch from the eggs.

STEP 2: The silkworms are fed mulberry leaves. The worms eat night and day until they grow very fat. During this period, they must be protected from drafts, loud noises, and strong smells.

STEP 3: The worms produce a jelly-like substance that hardens into a thin strand, or fiber, when it is exposed to air. For three or four days, the worms wrap themselves in this fiber until they have spun a cocoon around themselves. The cocoon looks like a puffy white ball.

STEP 4: The cocoons are kept in a dry place for eight or nine days. Then each cocoon is dipped in hot water to loosen the fiber. Once unwound, the fiber from one cocoon can be almost 1000 meters (3300 feet) long!

STEP 5: Five to eight fibers are twisted together to make one thread that is suitable for weaving into fabric. The thread can be dyed before or after weaving.

Silkmoth

Silkworms

Workers dye silk thread and then hang it up to dry.

How Silk Was Used

Silk was used for more than just fabric in ancient China. Because it is so strong, fishing lines and strings for bows were made from silk. It was even used to make a very special kind of paper.

Silk was so precious that it was eventually used for money. People used silk to pay taxes, and some government employees were paid with silk instead of gold.

The Silk Trade

When people in foreign countries first saw silk, they were eager to buy it and willing to pay large sums of money for it. Traders from ancient Rome made the long journey of over 6400 kilometers (4000 miles) to China to trade gold, silver, and gems for Chinese silk. Because so much silk traveled from China to Rome, the various trade routes became known as the Silk Road.

This silk embroidery was created during the Ming dynasty (1368–1644 CE).

福

The Secret Gets Out

When people from outside of China first saw silk cloth, they had no idea how it was made. It took them a long time to find out. In ancient China, death was the punishment for revealing the secret, or for trying to smuggle silkmoths, caterpillars or eggs out of the country. But eventually silkworm eggs and the secret of making silk spread to Korea, India, Italy, and other countries.

Silk Embroidery

Silk embroidery began in ancient times. The technique was used to decorate clothes, and also to create works of art, such as wall hangings.

One of the most famous Chinese art forms is double-sided silk embroidery. Most artistic embroidery pieces are meant to be viewed from just one side, but double-sided embroidery presents a beautiful image on both sides. To create this art form, embroiderers start with a piece of silk fabric that is almost transparent. The stitching is done with two needles, each threaded with a different color. In some cases, the silk threads used are extremely fine, less than one-tenth the width of a human hair. Working slowly and carefully, artists are able to create embroidery that shows the same image on both sides, sometimes with different colors in each image.

Silk in Modern Times

Today, silk is still a popular fabric for clothing. It is very comfortable to wear because it is soft and light. Silk clothing is warm in winter and cool in summer. Many silk fabrics reflect light, creating a soft, shimmering effect.

Silk is also used to make upholstery, window drapes, and bedding. As in ancient times, it is often expensive and is considered a luxury fabric.

China was not able to keep the method for making silk a secret, but it is still the world's leading silk producer. Even though there are over 30 countries that make silk, over half the world supply comes from China.

EVERYDAY INNOVATIONS

Many practical inventions from ancient China are still used today. Some have become beautiful arts and crafts, which continue to be admired and enjoyed around the world.

A carved lacquer cup for holding artists' paintbrushes

Lacquer

Lacquer is made from the sap of the lacquer tree. Some people call it the first plastic. It was painted on objects made of wood or bamboo to help preserve and protect them. Many practical items, such as kitchen utensils like chopsticks and bowls, were lacquer-coated so they could stand up to high heat and frequent use.

It was probably during the Shang dynasty (1650–1100 BCE) that the Chinese discovered lacquer, which later became available in many colors. Sometimes over 100 layers of lacquer were applied in order to create a thick coating in which artists could carve beautiful designs.

A porcelain plate from the Ming or Qing dynasty

Porcelain

Ordinary pottery is made when clay is molded into the desired shape and fired, or baked, in a kiln. Porcelain is made from a mixture of a white clay called kaolin, and powdered "China stone," a rock that contains the mineral feldspar. When this clay is fired at very high temperatures, it turns into porcelain. As well as being translucent (light shines through it), porcelain is harder and stronger than other kinds of pottery.

Early forms of porcelain were first made during the Tang dynasty (618–907 CE). By the end of the Yuan dynasty (1279–1368 CE), China had produced the fine porcelain we know today. The method for making porcelain was kept secret because porcelain objects were extremely valuable.

Marco Polo was the first person to use the word "china" for porcelain, as many people still do today.

Modern matches ignite from friction.

Matches

The Chinese invented the first matches, which were thin sticks of pine. Sulfur on the tips ignited quickly when touched to a flame. Matches (called "fire sticks" in Chinese) were useful for transferring a flame from one place to another.

Kite

The kite was invented in China as early as the 5th century BCE. By this time, silk had become available and was an ideal material for making kites, as well as the lines that controlled them. Later, kites were also made from paper.

Ancient and medieval Chinese texts list many uses for kites, such as measuring distances, testing wind, frightening the enemy in battle, and sending signals for military operations.

Nowadays, kite-making is still a craft and kite flying is a popular pastime.

A modern folding umbrella

Umbrella

Umbrellas provide both shade from the sun and shelter from the rain. The umbrellas we use today can be folded up when not in use. This type of umbrella was probably invented in China during the 1st century CE. The tops of the first umbrellas were made with thick oiled paper, which kept water out.

The Chinese character for umbrella is 伞, a pictograph that resembles the shape of a modern umbrella. (For more information on Chinese writing and pictographs, see page 42.)

Fishing Reel

A crank handle is used to turn a wheel. The Chinese invented the crank handle in the 2nd century BCE. This invention led to the first fishing reel.

Modern fishing reels still use a crank handle.

Toothbrush

Ancient civilizations cleaned their teeth with a "chew stick," a thin twig with a frayed end that was rubbed against the teeth. The first toothbrushes with bristles were invented in China in the late 1400s CE. The handle was either bone or bamboo, and the bristles were made from stiff hairs taken from a hog's neck.

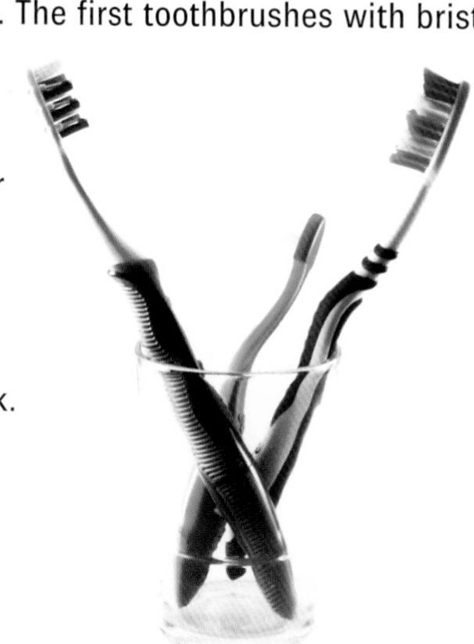

FOOD

Every culture has its favorite foods and ways of preparing special dishes. The ancient Chinese came up with some food inventions and innovations that have spread all around the world and are still popular today.

These Chinese workers are making "hand-sliced noodles."

Noodles

For a long time, people have argued about who invented noodles. Chinese, Italian, and Arab cultures all claim to be the first. But a recent discovery has put the argument to rest. Archaeologists working in northeastern China dug up an ancient bowl that had 4000-year-old thin, yellow noodles inside. These are the oldest noodles ever found.

Noodles have become one of China's favorite foods. The most common noodles are made from wheat flour and water, sometimes mixed with eggs. Some noodles are made from rice flour. One type of thin, clear noodle is made from mung beans.

Today, most noodles are made by machine, but some are still made by hand. For instance, "hand-sliced noodles" are made by cutting thin strips from a large ball of dough and letting them fall directly into a pot of boiling water.

Green Tea

The Chinese were probably the first to drink green tea. It is different from the tea that is traditionally served in Western countries, which is known as black tea.

Recently, green tea has become very popular around the world. Some people claim that drinking it may have health benefits.

Chopsticks

Chopsticks are popular eating utensils in East Asian countries. They were invented in China during the Shang dynasty (1650–1100 BCE). The oldest chopsticks ever found came from a tomb in China. They were made of bronze sometime around 1200 BCE.

Today, chopsticks are usually made from bamboo, wood, metal, or plastic. The Chinese call them *kuai-zi*, which means "quickly." At one time, the expression "chop-chop" meant "quickly," and this is how chopsticks got their English name.

Soybeans are used to make tofu (left), soy milk (center), and soy sauce (front). Tofu is used in many different dishes.

Tofu

Tofu, or bean curd, was invented in China. It is made from soy milk, in much the same way cheese is made from cow milk. First, dried soybeans are soaked until they turn soft. Then they are ground into a milky liquid, which is filtered and boiled. Salt or a mineral called gypsum is added to thicken the mixture and turn it into curds. The curds are pressed to remove excess water and form the tofu into blocks. Slightly different methods are used to produce various kinds of tofu. Some are as soft as jelly, while others are as firm as cheddar cheese.

Thousand-Year-Old Eggs

"Thousand-year-old eggs" or "century eggs" refer to preserved eggs, a popular Chinese food. Although the eggs are not as old as their names suggest, they do take a long time to make. Chicken, duck, or quail eggs may be used, although duck eggs are preferred.

To make these eggs, clay, ash, salt, rice straw, and a chemical called lime are mixed together to create a paste. Then a thick coat is applied to the eggs. After several weeks or months, the ingredients in the paste have soaked through the shells. When they are ready, the white of the eggs has turned brown and has a jelly-like consistency. The yolk is dark green and creamy.

Thousand-year-old eggs can be eaten uncooked and served on their own as a side dish. They also can be chopped up and added to dishes, or mixed into rice porridge to add flavor.

Salted Duck Eggs

Salted duck eggs are another preserved food invented by the Chinese. There are two ways of making them. Fresh eggs are soaked in a sealed jar filled with a salty liquid called brine, or the eggs are coated with a thick, salty paste and packed inside a container. They are then left for a period of weeks or months. When they are ready to be boiled or steamed, the egg whites have turned from clear to white, and the yolk is a reddish-orange color.

Salted duck eggs can be served on their own, chopped up with the shell peeled or left on, or added to other dishes. Despite the name, salted duck eggs can also be made using chicken eggs, although the texture and taste will be slightly different.

HEALTH AND HEALING

Chinese medicine has a long history. Its ancient methods of using acupuncture, herbs, and diet to treat and prevent disease are still used around the world.

Ginseng

Since ancient times, the Chinese have valued herbs to prevent and treat medical problems. One of these herbs is ginseng, which has become world famous.

Many people believe that the Chinese were the first to use ginseng. An ancient medical text reveals that this herb was being used as medicine 2000 years ago.

Some scientific studies have shown that ginseng does have positive effects, such as strengthening the body's immune system. However, more evidence is needed to prove some claims made about the benefits of this herb.

The root of the ginseng plant is used to prevent and treat illness.

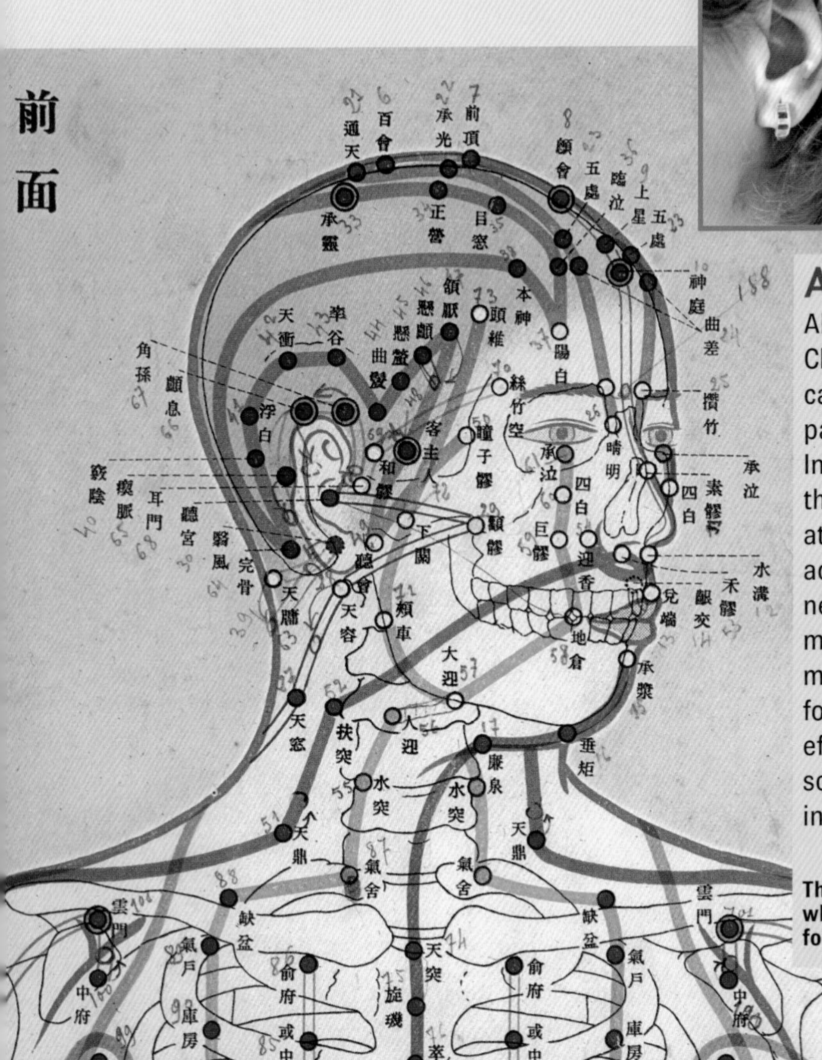

Acupuncture

About 2000 years ago, the Chinese developed a technique called acupuncture to treat pain and certain illnesses. In acupuncture treatment, the doctor inserts needles at specific places called acupoints. Different sizes of needles are used for different medical problems. Today, medical researchers have found that acupuncture is an effective method for treating some medical conditions, including pain.

This diagram shows the acupoints where needles might be inserted for acupuncture treatments.

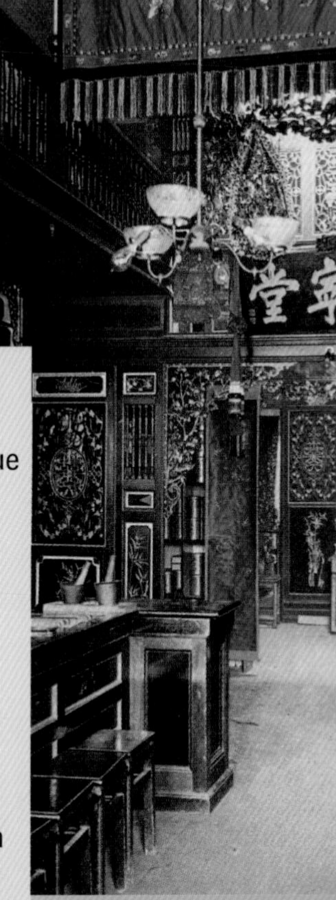

Traditional Chinese medicines were prepared in this California pharmacy at the beginning of the 1900s CE.

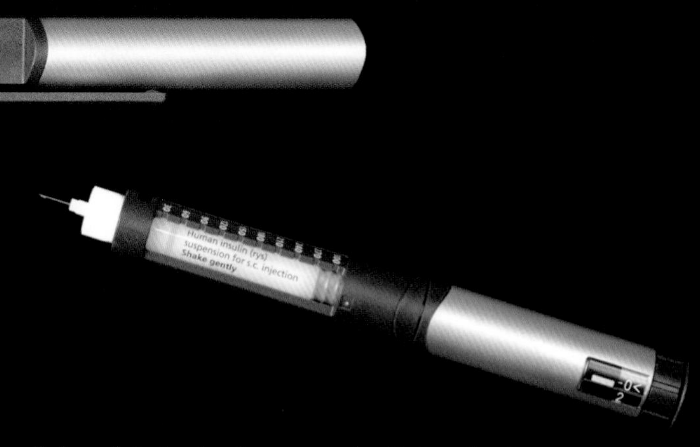
Today, diabetes is often treated with insulin. Some people use an insulin pen like this one to give themselves injections.

Treating Diabetes

The Chinese were probably the first people to diagnose diabetes. Patients with diabetes have a large amount of sugar in their urine, and the Chinese knew this by the 7th century CE. They recommended a diet that is similar to the one that today's doctors give to diabetic patients.

Curing Disease with Vitamins

Many diseases are caused by not having enough of a certain vitamin. While the ancient Chinese did not know about vitamins, they discovered effective ways to treat these diseases. As early as the 3rd century CE, Chinese authors were recommending that people eat specific foods to cure certain illnesses.

Modern science tells us that these authors were right. For example, a disease known as beriberi is caused by not getting enough Vitamin B1. The diets prescribed long ago for people with beriberi contain foods that are rich in this vitamin.

How did the Chinese know which foods to recommend? They probably learned by trial and error.

Carp contains Vitamin B1. Old Chinese texts recommend eating carp as a way to treat beriberi.

Inoculations

An inoculation is like a vaccination, an injection that protects you from getting a disease. A vaccination usually puts a dead virus into your body, and your immune system learns how to fight the virus. Then, if you are exposed to the live virus, your body is able to fight it off.

An inoculation uses a live virus, so there is some danger that the virus might cause disease. However, the ancient Chinese invented ways to minimize this danger. They used inoculations to fight smallpox in the 10th century CE, or possibly even earlier. But they did not use needles to give injections, as we do today. One of their methods was to put the virus on a piece of cotton and insert it into the patient's nose. In this way, some of the virus was breathed in, and some was absorbed through the skin inside the nostril.

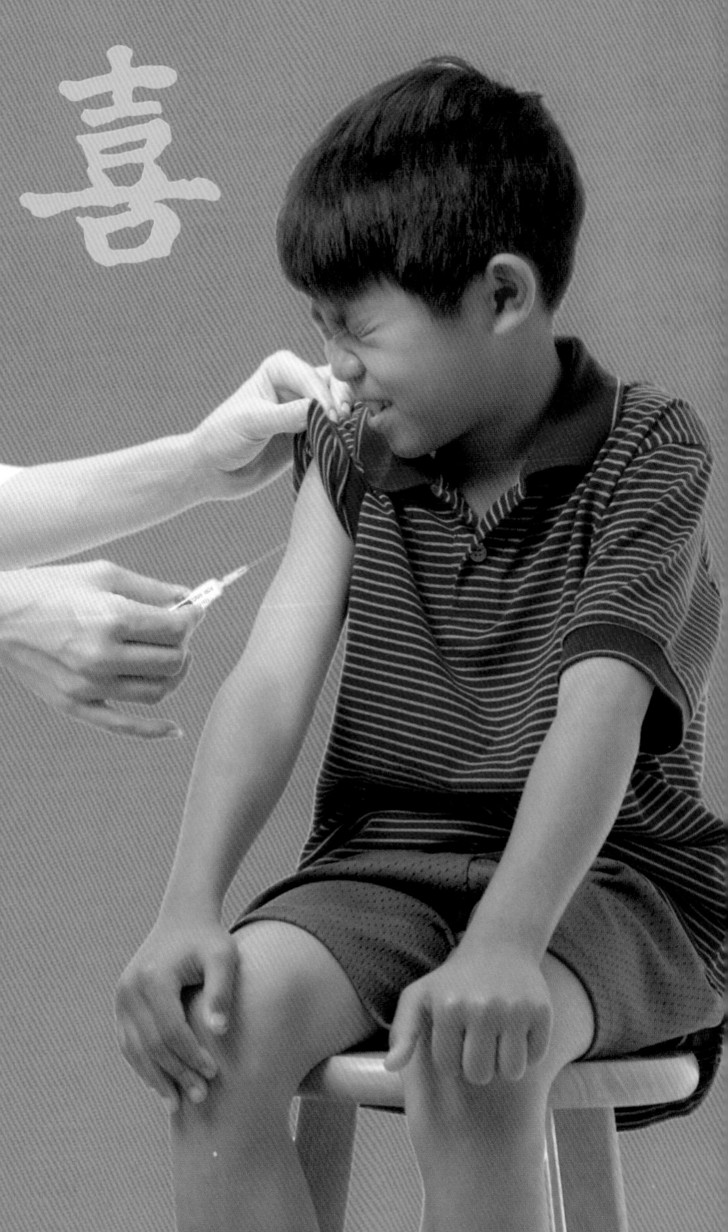

GAMES AND SPORTS

Many games and sports were invented during China's long history. Some of these are still played today and others have changed over time.

Zu-qiu

Zu-qiu, which means "kick the ball," is an ancient Chinese game similar to today's soccer. Some historians believe that this game was invented by an emperor over 4000 years ago as a way to train soldiers.

During the Han dynasty (207 BCE–220 CE), *zu-qiu* became a popular form of entertainment for the imperial courts. At that time, there were three crescent-shaped goals at each end of the field, and the players could score points by kicking the ball into any of the six goals. The balls were made from animal skin stuffed with hair. Balls filled with air were used in the late Tang dynasty (618–907 CE).

In China today, *zu-qiu* refers to modern soccer, which is extremely popular around the world.

Right: A game of *zu-qiu* during the Ming dynasty

Old playing cards

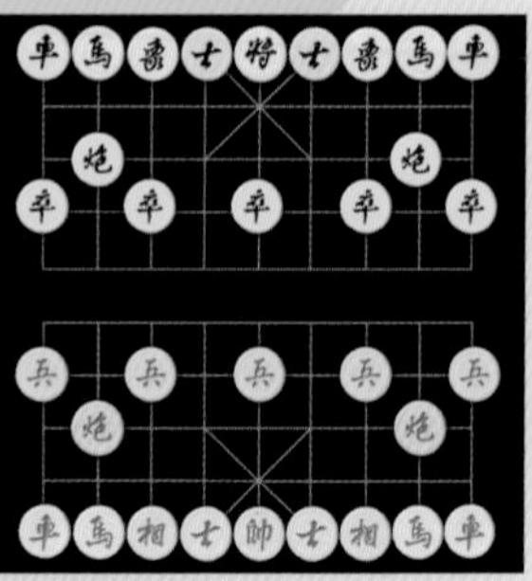

***Xiang-qi* playing board**

Playing Cards

Playing cards were invented in China by the 9th century CE, after paper and woodblock printing had become available (see Paper and Printing, page 24). But they were smaller and narrower than the cards we play with today. There were 30 cards in a deck instead of 52, and just three suits: coins, strings of coins, and stacks of coins. Even today, some cards used in China still have the coin designs, which are similar to those in the game of *ma-jiang* (see next page).

Xiang-qi

Xiang-qi, which is known in the West as "Chinese chess," is a strategy board game played in China since about 700 CE. It is similar to Western chess. The game is based on a military battle. In the modern version, each player has 16 pieces, including one general and five soldiers. The object of Chinese chess is to capture the opponent's general.

Ma-jiang

Ma-jiang, also known outside China as mah-jong, is a game played by four people. Some historians believe that it was developed in the early Ming dynasty (1368–1644 CE). The game requires skill, strategy, careful observation, and a good memory. It is similar to a card game, but played with hard tiles engraved with Chinese characters and symbols, and divided into suits, like playing cards.

During the 20th century, *ma-jiang* was banned for a time in China because people were using the game to gamble. But it has once again become popular there, and is played around the world. Many people enjoy *ma-jiang* without betting money.

In recent times, *ma-jiang* has become popular once again.

Wei-qi

The Chinese invented the game of *wei-qi* over 2500 years ago. It is better known around the world as Go, which is the Japanese name for the game.

Wei-qi is played by two people using black and white pieces on a board divided into squares. The object of the game is to surround and then remove the opponent's pieces. *Wei-qi* requires skill and strategy, but it is not difficult to learn.

A 19th-century game of *wei-qi*

An ancient game of *chui-wan*

Chui-wan

Chui-wan, which means "strike the ball," was an outdoor game, similar to golf, played in ancient China. The players scored points by using a stick to hit a ball into a hole in the ground. The game had become very popular by the time of the Song dynasty (960–1279 CE). Some people believe the modern sport of golf was developed from *chui-wan*.

CHINA TODAY

Today's China is still a land where amazing innovations take place and develop into new technologies. It has become a modern nation. During the last two decades, I have returned to China many times, and on each visit I saw the changes with my own eyes.

I was born and grew up in Purple Sunshine Lane, a quiet neighborhood of two-level buildings in central Shanghai. These typical row houses were built in the early 1900s. Throughout my childhood, Shanghai's Park Hotel, with 24 floors, was the tallest building in China. My classmates and I would sometimes walk to Nanjing Road to admire the hotel, which seemed so tall it touched the sky. In the spring of 2005, Purple Sunshine Lane was torn down by dozens of bulldozers. Within two years, it was replaced by a cluster of expensive high-rise condominiums. Each of them is taller than the Park Hotel! People in Shanghai used to call a building with 6 floors a high-rise, but now you can see hundreds of apartment buildings and office towers with more than 30 floors.

All over China's larger cities, skyscrapers have spread like mushrooms after a spring rain.

China is the largest country in the world, with a population of 1.3 billion. Over 100 cities have more than 1 million residents. The 4 largest cities have more than 10 million each. One in five people in the world is Chinese.

Chinese engineers continue to build beautiful and innovative bridges. The Lupu Bridge in Shanghai, 3.9 kilometers (2.4 miles) long, is the world's longest segmental arch bridge. It was constructed in 2003. Hangzhou Bay Bridge, completed

Top: The skyline in the city of Shenzen
MIddle: Shanghai at night
Bottom: The Xupu Bridge in Shanghai

in May 2008, is the longest sea-crossing bridge in the world. It is 36 kilometers (22 miles) in length. The Sutong Bridge, the world's longest cable-stayed bridge, stretches for 1 kilometer (0.7 miles) over the Yangtze River.

China has a large superhighway network that connects much of the country. In big cities, there are subway systems, high-speed trains, light rail transit, and magnetic trains.

Left: A magnetic levitation train
Bottom: A Chinese subway train

CHINA TODAY *continued*

The Chinese launched manned space flights in 2003, 2005, and 2008. Their latest mission sent three astronauts into space and included the first Chinese space walk. China also designs and builds passenger airplanes.

Five countries in the world have nuclear weapons. China is one of them.

The country has also developed into an industrial power. It produces 33 percent of the world's steel, and over 60 percent of the world's photocopiers, microwave ovens, and DVD players. More than 40 percent of our household appliances, toys, clothes, and shoes are made there. Take a look in the dollar stores in your neighborhood—you'll find that most of the goods there are made in China.

The Chinese produce many other high-tech goods, such as computer parts, cell phones, and digital cameras. They have built the largest water-driven electric power generator in the world at the Three Gorges Dam on the Yangtze River. It supplies about 10 percent of the country's electric power. For an Arctic expedition in 2008, China developed its own robot, named the "North Pole ARV." It monitors the Arctic Ocean and carries scientific equipment.

A Chinese space rocket

Right and below: The Three Gorges Dam

Above: China's National Olympic Stadium

Left: China competes against USA in basketball at the 2008 Olympics.

Right: Figure skaters Quing Pang and Jian Tong

In sports, Chinese athletes shine brightly. Basketball fans know Yao Ming from the NBA. Chinese divers, gymnasts, and figure skaters have won medals everywhere. China held its first Summer Olympic Games in 2008 in Beijing.

China has a long history of innovation and invention, and its contribution to the world is far from over.

A Note on the Chinese Language

The earliest samples of Chinese writing are from the Shang dynasty (1650–1100 BCE). The first emperor of the Qin dynasty (221–207 BCE) standardized the writing system throughout the empire.

The Chinese language is known as Mandarin outside China, but in China it is called *pu-tong-hua,* which means "common speech." *Pinyin*, which means "spelling sound," is a system that uses the same letters as English to help people pronounce Mandarin words.

Written Chinese words are referred to as characters. Some are called pictographs because they give a picture of an object, for example:

Some characters are called ideographs because they represent an idea, for example:

Sometimes two characters are combined to create a new meaning, for example:

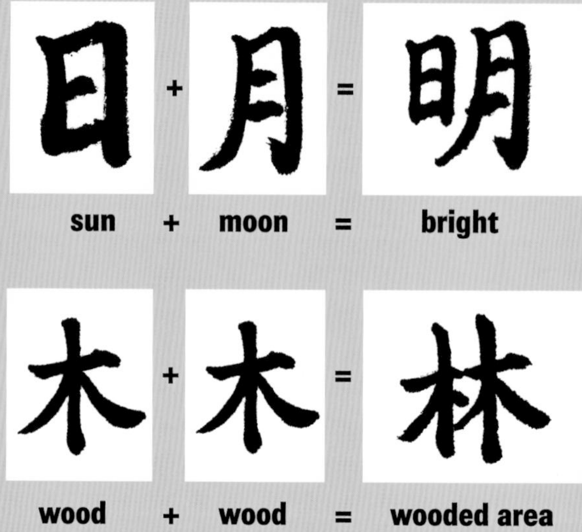

Many Chinese living in Canada and the United States speak Cantonese, which is a southern dialect of Chinese. Around the world, there are about 70 million people who speak Cantonese, while over 1.2 billion speak Mandarin.

Chinese characters appear throughout the pages in this book. Below, you will find the meaning of each of these characters.

Further Reading

Bailey, Linda. *Adventures in Ancient China.* Toronto: Kids Can Press, 2004.

Beshore, George. *Science in Ancient China.* Madison, WI: Turtleback Books, 1998.

Challen, Paul. *Life in Ancient China.* New York: Crabtree, 2005.

Cotterell, Arthur. *Ancient China.* New York: DK Publishing, 2005.

Deady, Kathleen, and Muriel Dubois. *Ancient China.* Mankato, MN: Capstone Press, 2004.

Steele, Philip. *The Chinese Empire (Passport to the Past series).* New York: Rosen Publishing, 2009.

Williams, Brian. *Ancient China.* New York: Viking, 1996.

Williams, Suzanne. *Made in China: Ideas and Inventions from Ancient China.* Berkeley, CA: Pacific View Press, 1996.

Selected Sources

Bai, Shouyi, ed. *An Outline History of China.* Beijing: The Foreign Language Press, 1982.

Huang, Ray. *1587, A Year of No Significance: The Ming Dynasty in Decline.* New Haven, CT: Yale University Press, 1981.

Hucker, Charles O. *China's Imperial Past: An Introduction to Chinese History and Culture.* Stanford, CA: Stanford University Press, 1997.

Needham, Joseph. *Science in Traditional China.* Cambridge, MA: Harvard University Press, 1981.

Temple, Robert. *The Genius of China: 3,000 Years of Science, Discovery and Invention.* Rochester, VT: Inner Traditions, 2007.

Thomas, Roy. *China: The Awakening Giant.* Toronto: McGraw-Hill Ryerson, 1981.

Zhao, Hai-ming, and Jing-sheng Xu. *China's Ancient Inventions: Words and Pictures.* Beijing: Beijing Library Press, 1999.

Credits

Front cover top, Richard Cano; **front cover middle,** 45RPM; **front cover bottom, 34 middle,** Murat Koc; **1, 2, 4, 5 bottom right, 12–13 background, 12 bottom left, 43 both, 47, back cover top right, back cover bottom right,** Qizhi He; **5 top right, 6–7 top, back cover middle background,** zubin li; **5 top left, 28 middle right,** Merrymoonmary; **5 middle left, 34 top,** yungshu chao; **8 top, 23 background,** best-photo; **8 bottom,** KingWu; **9 bottom,** Laurence Gough; **13 bottom right, 33 background,** YinYang; **14 top,** Yali Shi; **15 top,** rest; **15 top background, 31 middle background, 32 bottom background,** Rob Broek; **15 bottom background,** jiaxi shen; **16 top main,** Jason Bradley; **16 top inset,** Greg McCracken; **17 top background,** Baris Onal; **17 top inset,** Furchin; **19 bottom, 20 bottom background,** archives; **24 background, 25 bottom, 26 top background,** IssueKid; **27 bottom right,** Gregory Lang; **27 top background,** Dexter Mikami; **27 bottom background,** Anneclaire Le Royer; **28 top left,** Vickie Sichau; **28 bottom left,** Jaime Roset; **28 bottom left background,** Izabela Habur; **28 background,** studiovision; **29 top,** Giorgio Fochesato; **29 bottom,** Joris van den Heuvel; **29 left and right background,** Jamie Carroll; **30 bottom,** fabphoto; **32 top background,** Anna Yu; **32 middle right inset,** Skip ODonnell; **32 bottom right inset,** Ivan Mateev; **32 left inset,** Vyacheslav Anyakin; **33 top left,** Igor Dutina; **36 middle right, back cover fourth left,** Hector Joseph Lumang; **38 middle,** Xin Zhu; **38 bottom, 39 top, 39 background,** Alex Nikada. All ©iStockphoto Inc.

3, 9 top right, 13 bottom left, 14 middle, 18 top, 18 bottom inset, 21 top inset, 21 middle inset, 35 bottom left. All ©2009 Jupiterimages Corporation.

Chinese characters throughout book, 5 bottom left, 16 bottom both, 19 middle, 23 bottom right, 26 middle and bottom, 32 top right inset, back cover second left, ©Ting-xing Ye.

5 middle right, back cover top left, Szefei; **6 middle,** Paul Merrett; **6 bottom,** Gary718; **7 middle,** Amy Harris; **7 bottom,** Himiko2023909; **9 left,** Miao; **12 top left,** Swisshippo; **12 bottom right,** Lihui; **13 top,** Flashon; **20 top,** Jorisvo; **21 top main,** Mingtakucl; **21 bottom main,** Hyugo; **21 bottom inset,** William Howell; **22 bottom,** Hou Guima; **25 bottom,** Eric Gevaert; **26 top,** Rodho; **27 top left, back cover bottom left,** Magicsea; **27 middle left,** Summersky; **27 bottom left,** Phaif; **27 top right,** Mudong; **31 top left,** Greedypanda; **31 middle inset,** Tihis; **31 bottom left,** Litoff; **31 bottom right,** Ivan Kmit; **33 bottom left,** Shariff Che' Lah; **33 top right, back cover third left,** Howard Hong; **33 bottom right,** Alvin Teo; **35 top left,** Joel Iedema; **35 right,** Geotrac; **36 top inset,** Sprinter81; **36 bottom,** Seesea; **37 top left,** Feng Hui; **37 top right background,** Saniphoto; **37 bottom background,** Donkeyru; **38 top,** Bartlomiej Magierowski; **38 top background,** Sofiaworld; **39 middle,** Holger Mette; **39 bottom,** Matt Grant; **40 top,** Wayne Zhou; **40 middle and bottom,** Aschwin Prein; **41 top,** Tr0020032; **41 right,** Olga Besnard; **41 left,** Wanghanan. All ©Dreamstime.com.

14 bottom, *Qing Ming Shang He Tu* or *Along the river at the Qingming Spring festival*, 1736 replica of 12th century northern Song scroll, China, detail. National Palace Museum, Taiwan; **15 bottom,** Cheng Chi, Yuan dynasty, 13th–14th century AD, China. Freer Gallery of Art; **17 bottom,** print from *Hsin I Hsiang Fa Yoo*; **19 top,** Eileen Tweedy; **23 top right,** Tang dynasty, China. Musée Guimet, Paris/Gianni Dagli Orti; **24 right**; **24 left,** 1374, Ming dynasty, China; **25 top,** Mottahedah Collection; **28 top right,** Period of Northern Dynasties, 551 AD, from grave in Turfan, Xinjiang, China. Genius of China Exhibition; **28 bottom right,** Golestan Palace, Teheran/Gianni Dagli Orti; **30 top,** National Palace Museum, Taiwan/HarperCollins Publishers; **30 middle,** *Three heroes of the Water Margin*, or *Outlaw of the Marshes*, Ching or Manchu dynasty, China. Musée Guimet, Paris/Gianni Dagli Orti; **31 top right,** Private Collection/Marc Charmet; **34 bottom,** Private Collection/Gianni Dagli Orti. All ©The Art Archive.

15 middle, detail from cover by David Craig. **17 middle,** Chang Heng, Han Dynasty. Clive Streeter ©Dorling Kindersley, Courtesy of The Science Museum; **18 middle,** Geoff Brightling ©Dorling Kindersley, Courtesy of the Pitt Rivers Museum, University of Oxford; **18 bottom main,** Chen Chao ©Dorling Kindersley; **22 top,** Dave King ©Dorling Kindersley, Courtesy of The Science Museum, London; **36 middle left,** Geoff Brightling ©Dorling Kindersley. **20 bottom,** assiewin/Stockxpert. **23 both left,** ©Photo by Vlasta Radan; Book repository: Special Collections & Archives, University of California, Riverside. **29 middle,** Werner Forman/Art Resource, NY. **34–35,** Yale Collection of Western Americana, Beinecke Rare Book and Manuscript Library. **36 top background,** *Outlaws of the Marsh*, ca. 15th century. **37 top right,** *Kada hone o kezurite kan'u yakizu o ryōji suru zu* by Kuniyoshi Utagawa, 1853. Library of Congress, LC-DIG-jpd-02612. **37 bottom,** ©CLARO CORTES IV/Reuters/Corbis.

Index

TING-XING YE was born and raised in Shanghai, China. Since the day she won the privilege of having her own library card, she has loved reading books. Events in China made it difficult for her to fulfill her childhood dream of going to university, but eventually she succeeded. She graduated from Beijing University with a degree in English Literature, and worked for seven years as a government interpreter before coming to Canada as a Visiting Scholar at York University.

In Canada, Ting-xing began to write, supporting herself by working as an office clerk and baby-sitter. She published her memoir, *A Leaf in the Bitter Wind*, in 1997, and followed it with three picture books and a chapter book before writing her young adult novels, *Throwaway Daughter* and *Mountain Girl, River Girl*. Ting-xing's young adult non-fiction book, *My Name Is Number 4*, describes her life in China during the Cultural Revolution.

Ting-xing lives in Orillia, Ontario.

Also in Annick's acclaimed We Thought of It series:

- ★ "The Year's Best" List, *Resource Links*
- ★ Children's Non-Fiction Top 10 List, Ontario Library Association
- ★ *Best Books for Kids & Teens 2008*, starred selection, Canadian Children's Book Centre
- ★ 2008 Skipping Stones Honor Award
- ★ 2008/2009 Hackmatack Children's Choice Book Award finalist
- ★ 2009 Rocky Mountain Book Award finalist
- ★ Silver Birch Award 2009 nomination

"... chock-a-block full of interesting information and pictures." —*CM Magazine*

"[An] informative and easy to read book ... attractive and useful." —*Children's Book News*

- ★ *Best Books for Kids & Teens 2009*, Canadian Children's Book Centre

" ... deserves a permanent spot on any reader's bookshelf ... "—*ForeWord*

"A real eye-opener to enlighten children and adults alike ... " —*Resource Links*

Go to www.annickpress.com to view book trailers for these and other exciting titles.

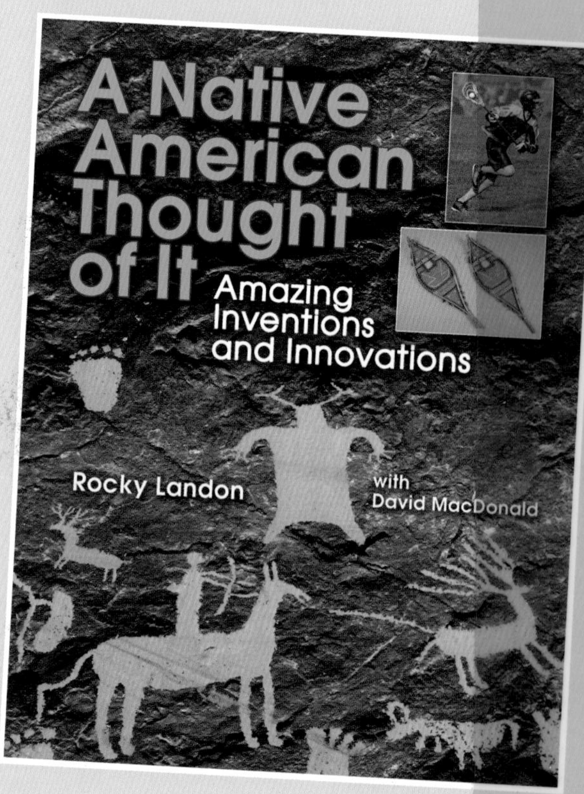